Your Senses

Written by Sally Morgan

Contents

Your five senses

Seeing, hearing, touching, smelling and tasting. These are your five senses. Without them, you wouldn't be able to see or hear, feel the things you touch, sniff the air, or taste food.

FACT
As we get older, our senses get weaker, and we do not see, hear or taste as well.

Our senses are in action from the moment we're born and we use them to explore and learn about the world around us. Everybody has the same five senses, but some people have better senses than others. For example, they have sharper vision or can hear more sounds.

Sense organs

You have five sense organs – eyes, ears, skin, nose and tongue.

Sense organs are connected to your nervous system. The nervous system is made up of your brain, spinal cord and nerves. Nerves are long and thread-like. They're found in your arms and legs, head and inside your body, carrying information to and from your brain and spinal cord.

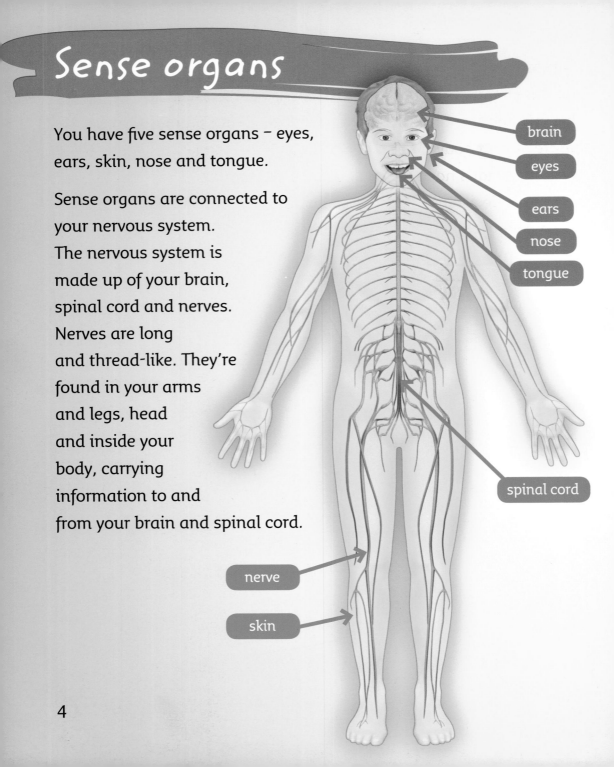

brain

eyes

ears

nose

tongue

spinal cord

nerve

skin

Your sense organs gather information all the time, even when you're not thinking about it, for example smells and sounds. They send this information along nerves to your brain. Your brain is the control centre of your body. It uses information from your sense organs to work out what's happening and to make decisions. These could be important decisions such as jumping out of the way of something, or moving your hand from a hot object.

Some smells can be very strong and your nose sends this information back to your brain.

5

Seeing the world

We need light to see. Light enters your eye through your pupil, the black spot in the middle of your eye. When the light is dim, your pupil is large, so that lots of light can enter. But when the light is bright, your pupil is small to stop too much light getting in and damaging your eye.

Light passes through your pupil and falls on the back of your eye, where information is sent to your brain. Your brain uses the information to build a picture of what you see.

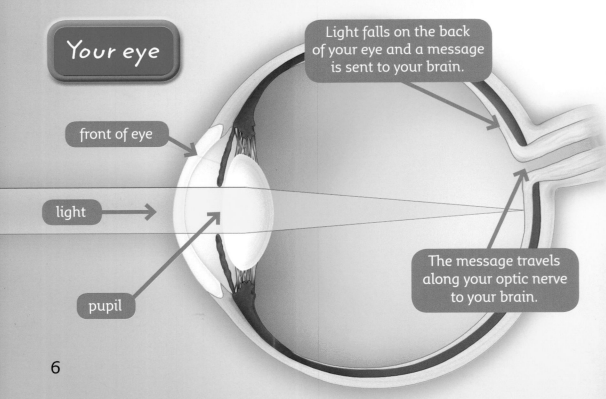

Your eye

Light falls on the back of your eye and a message is sent to your brain.

front of eye

light

pupil

The message travels along your optic nerve to your brain.

Each eye sees a slightly different picture. Your brain takes the two pictures and puts them together to produce one **3D** picture. This means you can judge how far away something is and you can pick up objects and play sport.

A colourful world

We can see in colour, unlike many animals that see only in shades of black and white.

However, we can only see colour when there's lots of light. At night, if we go outside in the dark, we can only see in black and white. When we first step into the dark, we can't see much, but after a while our eyes **adjust** and we can see more detail.

In daylight you can see colours and all the leaves in the tree, but at night all you can see is an outline of the tree.

Some people are colour-blind. This means they're unable to tell the difference between some colours, especially red and green. This is because their eyes can't detect some colours.

Hearing sounds

Sounds are all around you and you use your ears to hear them.

Sounds are made when something **vibrates**. For example, a guitar makes a sound when its strings are plucked.

Your ears collect the sounds and send them into a tube called an ear canal. They reach your eardrum and make it vibrate. The vibrations pass to your cochlea. This is a fluid-filled tube that is coiled just like a snail's shell. Inside your cochlea, the liquid moves tiny hairs that send messages along nerves to your brain. Your brain works out what the sounds are and where they came from.

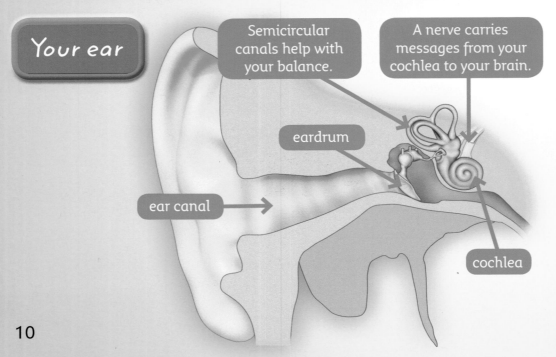

Your ear

Semicircular canals help with your balance.

A nerve carries messages from your cochlea to your brain.

eardrum

ear canal

cochlea

10

Your ears help you to balance too, using the semicircular canals near your cochlea. When you move your head, liquid inside the canals moves too. It pushes on hairs that send information to your brain. This tells your brain about the position of your head. At the same time, your eyes are sending information to your brain. Your brain uses all this information to move your arms and legs and stop you falling over.

When you spin around, lots of messages from your eyes and ears are sent to your brain, which gets confused and you feel giddy.

High and low sounds

We can hear different types of sounds. Some sounds are very high notes and others are low notes.

FACT
There are some sounds that no human can hear, such as the squeaky sounds made by bats and mice.

Young people have much better hearing than older people. They can hear high notes that older people can't.
Once people reach their 20s, they start to lose hairs in their cochlea so that they're unable to hear as many sounds.

Sound can be dangerous. Loud sounds made by jet engines and machinery or loud music damage the hairs and can cause hearing loss.

A hearing aid makes sounds louder so that people can hear them.

Feeling things

Your sense of touch allows you to feel your surroundings. You touch the food you eat, the clothes you wear and the things you pick up.

Your skin contains lots of nerve endings. There are different types of nerve endings. Some feel pain, others feel heat, cold or **pressure**. When these nerve endings sense something, such as the heat of a hot object, they send a message along your nerve to your brain.

Your skin

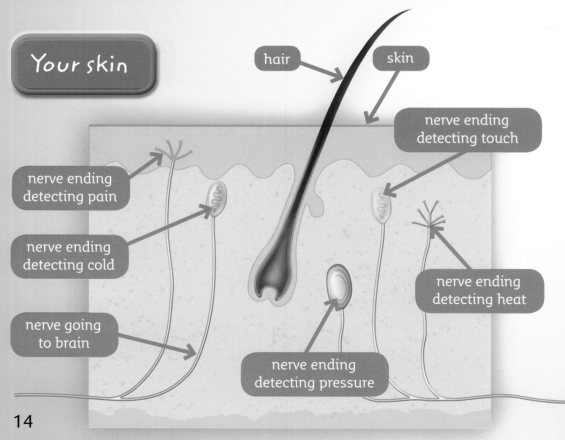

hair

skin

nerve ending detecting touch

nerve ending detecting pain

nerve ending detecting cold

nerve ending detecting heat

nerve going to brain

nerve ending detecting pressure

Some parts of your skin have better touch than others. This is because they have more nerve endings. The most **sensitive** skin covers your fingertips and lips while the thick skin that covers the soles of your feet doesn't feel much.

Your fingertips can feel the softness of a rabbit's fur.

Protecting us

When you touch something sharp, such as a needle, nerve endings in your skin feel the pain and send a warning message. This goes to your spinal cord and instantly a message is sent back telling your arm to pull your finger away.

This is called a **reflex**. You have no control over reflexes. They happen without you thinking about it and protect you from harm. There are many different types of reflex. For example, you blink when something flies towards your eyes and you hold up your arm to protect your face.

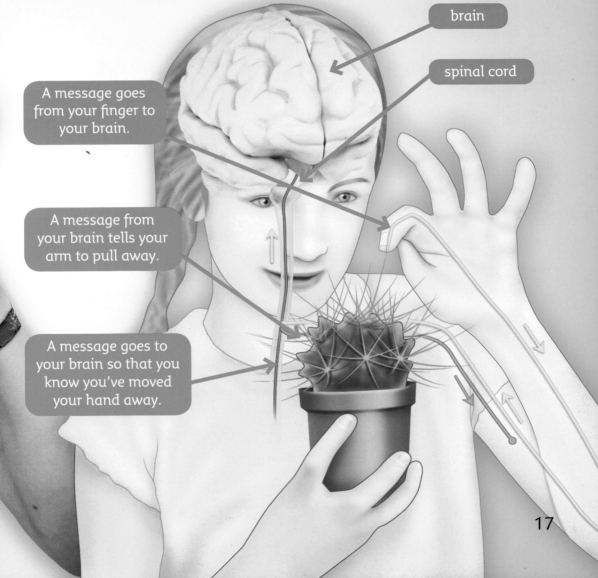

brain

spinal cord

A message goes from your finger to your brain.

A message from your brain tells your arm to pull away.

A message goes to your brain so that you know you've moved your hand away.

Sniffing smells

Smells are carried in the air and are pulled into your nose when you breathe.

Inside your nose are many small tubes lined with tiny hairs, each connected to a nerve. The hairs are covered in smell **detectors**. When the hairs are tickled by smells, the detectors sense the smell and send a message along a nerve to your brain. Then your brain recognises the smell.

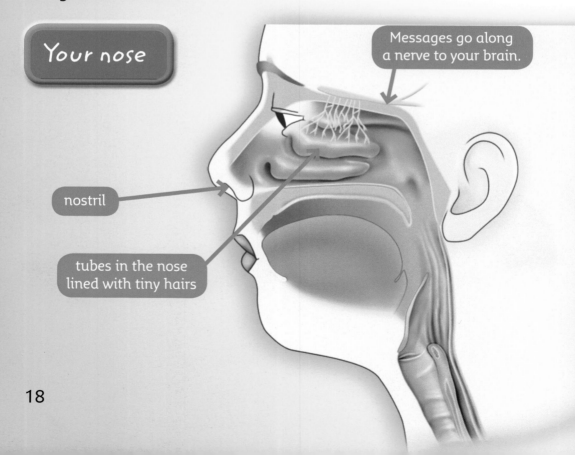

Your nose

Messages go along a nerve to your brain.

nostril

tubes in the nose lined with tiny hairs

Your nose is packed with about 5 million detectors and we can identify as many as 10,000 different smells. But this is not as good as a dog. A dog's nose is filled with 220 million detectors or more and a sense of smell thousands of times better than our own.

Different types of smells

Smells can warn us of danger, such as fire or gas, or food that has gone off. Smells can be nice too, like perfumed soaps and shampoos.

People have memories of smells that they grew up with or from holidays, for example, the smell of the sea, the scent of a flower or unpleasant farmyard smells. Smells can make us hungry too. When we smell food being cooked, we feel hungry.

Tasting food

You taste using your tongue. There are only five different tastes –
sweet, sour, bitter, salt and a savoury taste called umami.
It's the mix of these tastes, together with their smell and **texture**
that produces all the different **flavours** of food.

The surface of your tongue is covered in lots of tiny bumps.
These are called taste buds. Each taste bud is covered in tiny hairs.
The hairs sense the taste and send a message along nerves to your
brain, which recognises it. As you get older you lose taste buds and
you can't taste so well.

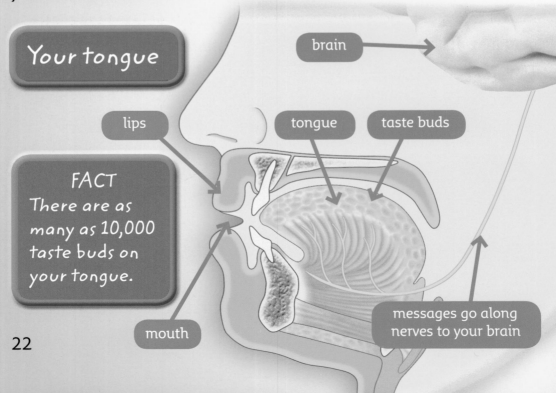

Your tongue

brain

lips

tongue

taste buds

FACT
There are as
many as 10,000
taste buds on
your tongue.

messages go along
nerves to your brain

mouth

Smell and supertasters

You need your sense of smell to taste properly. When you eat, you breathe in the smell of the food. The smell and taste of the food produce flavours in your mouth. If your nose is blocked because you have a cold, your sense of taste is very poor and food seems tasteless.

Supertasters have a much better sense of taste than other people. They have more taste buds and a better sense of smell. About one in every four people is a supertaster. Supertasters are often fussy about their food. They don't like strongly flavoured foods such as coffee, cabbage and spinach because they find the tastes too powerful.

FACT
Chilli peppers taste hot because the nerve endings in your mouth that detect pain can feel the heat of the chilli. It's not your taste buds!

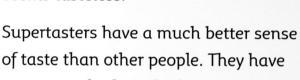

23

Inside your body

Your senses tell us about changes that are going on inside your body too. For example, they let you know if you're hungry or thirsty.

You feel thirsty when there's too little water in your blood. Your brain detects the lack of water and sends a message to your mouth to make you feel thirsty and want to drink.

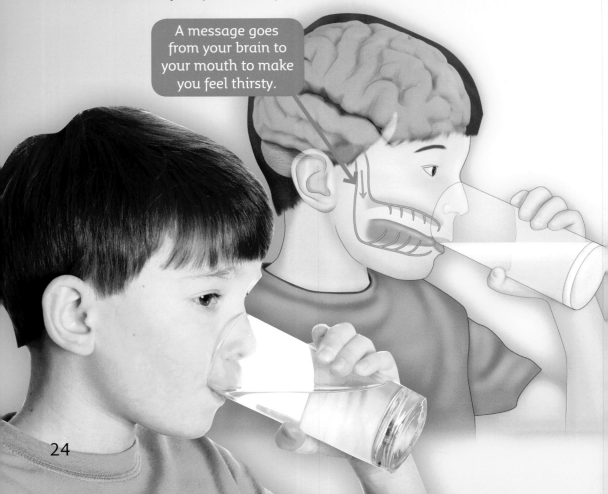

A message goes from your brain to your mouth to make you feel thirsty.

Your senses also tell you about pain in your body. Toothache is a warning that something is wrong with a tooth. For example, if you have tooth **decay**, nerve endings inside your tooth feel pain and your tooth aches.

A message goes from your tooth to your brain to make you feel pain.

25

Your senses are essential to your daily life. They tell you about your surroundings and warn you of danger. With your senses, you can see a colourful world with sounds and smells.

Glossary

3D   three-dimensional, having a feeling of depth

adjust   make small changes

decay   a hole in a tooth

detectors   something such as the end of a nerve that can pick up a signal, or respond to a change, for example detect smells or light

flavours   tastiness of food

pressure   pushing, pressing on something

reflex   an automatic and immediate reaction

sensitive   needing the lightest of touches

texture   the feel of something

vibrates   moves backwards and forwards very quickly while shaking

Index

What your senses do

You see with your eyes.

You touch with your skin.

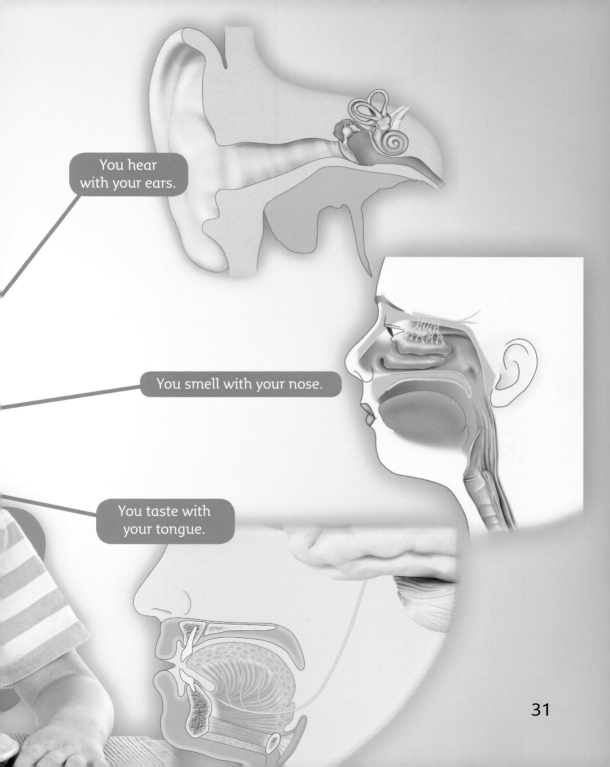

You hear with your ears.

You smell with your nose.

You taste with your tongue.

31

Ideas for reading

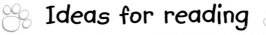

Written by Clare Dowdall BA(Ed), MA(Ed)
Lecturer and Primary Literacy Consultant

Learning objectives: read independently and with increasing fluency longer and less familiar texts; explain organizational features of texts; use syntax and context to build their store of vocabulary when reading for meaning; explain ideas and processes using imaginative and adventurous vocabulary and non-verbal gestures to support communication

Curriculum links: Science

Interest words: organs, supertasters, cochlea, nerve, reflex

Word count: 1,697

Resources: whiteboard, range of foods for tasting, pencils and paper

Getting started

- Ask children to close their eyes and sit quietly in order to notice what they can hear and smell. Discuss the things that they like to smell and listen to.

- Explain that they are going to read an information book about their senses. List all the senses that the children know on a whiteboard, and prompt them where needed. Ask children to suggest why they think that their senses are important and how they might work.

- Look at the front cover. Ask children to describe what senses the child in the photograph is using.

Reading and responding

- Read down through the contents and identify new words, e.g. organs, supertasters. Help children to read and understand these words. Remind children about using the glossary to help understand new words. Read through the glossary words to support children with pronunciation.

- Walk through the book and identify the features that provide additional information, e.g. diagrams and fact boxes.

- Read pp2–3 together. Discuss what the phrase "sharper vision" means and ask children to give an example of a job or hobby that needs sharp vision.